Unleash Your Creative Mindset

Jaime Vendera

Vendera
Publishing

Unleash Your Creative Mindset

Vendera Publishing
ISBN: 978-1-936307-12-8

Cover Design by Molly Burnside
www.crosssidedesigns.com

Interior Layout & Design by Scribe Freelance
www.scribefreelance.com

Edited by
Rich Dalglish

OTHER BOOKS BY JAIME VENDERA
AVAILABLE AT VENDERAPUBLISHING.COM

*I dedicate this book
To my wife and soul mate,*

DIANE VENDERA

*Without you,
I would not be driven to success.
You are that
"Special Something"
that instills within me
the passion, drive, and desire
that I feel every day
to perform, write, teach, and succeed.*

I love you.

ATTENTION ALL MINDSET USERS!

I invite each of you to become a member of the Mindset community. Please visit jaimevendera.com. Click on the Members link to enter. Next, click on the Unleash Your Creative Mindset link. The password to enter the members section is "superconscious."

Through the Mindset Members area you have access to the message board, where you can ask questions, offer answers, and share your creative Mindset experiences, letting friends know of your creative success.

Downloadable materials are also available on the Members section. These include a Mindset journal and a one-page Mindset layout for quick reference (thanks, Pam) with more materials to come. Join the Mindset community today!

Before you begin the Mindset journey, I would like to state that although the techniques described in this book are for boosting your creativity and your motivational drive, they have a spiritual background in nature. Although you do not need a belief in God for the Mindset program to work, God *is* the amplifier. Adding God and prayer to the Mindset program is like adding a turbo booster to the creative process, enhancing the likelihood of your creative success a hundredfold.

Note: I've learned a lot about the Mindset program since I originally released *Mindset: Programming Your Mind for Success*, which is why I've rewritten/retitled the book. So be forewarned: You are about to unlock the floodgates to your creativity. Let's proceed.

Contents

Before beginning this journey
I want to thank my mother,

LINDA FAGAN,

For always teaching me
To think outside the box,
Encouraging my dreams,
Supporting me in my beliefs,
&
Allowing me to spread my wings and fly.

I Love You.

Introducing Mindset

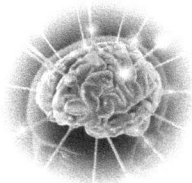

WOULDN'T IT BE GREAT to flip a switch to turn your mind into a perpetual idea generator, stimulate your motivational drive, eliminate writer's block, inspire a musical masterpiece, solve seemingly unsolvable problems, and offer solutions to your deepest questions?

My name is Jaime Vendera, and I've discovered that switch. I call it the Mindset program. By using this program, I've become a singer, vocal coach, author, publisher, glass-shattering world record holder, and television personality. I've written multiple nonfiction books on singing, self-publishing, and online teaching; produced dozens of fiction books; filmed countless instructional audio and video programs; and developed software. And I'm just getting started.

Ideas flow to me continuously. I cannot shut the creative process off, nor would I want to. I literally dream new ideas night after night, and I can show you how to do the same by tapping into that vault of creativity that lives within our minds, which I call the creative mindset. Once you tap into your creative mindset, ideas will flow like water.

Many of you may have experienced the creative mindset in the past, coming up with creative ideas seemingly out of nowhere, whether it be an angelic song, an idea for a revolutionary new product, or simply a creative approach to enhance your way of living. Some of you may have even experienced the fruits of your creative ideas as they unfolded, while others failed to maintain the motivational drive to see a single creative idea through to completion.

Trust me, I've been there. Before I developed this program, I had several great ideas, but they never made it past the thought process.

But that ended with the creation of the Mindset program. I've been fulfilling my creative ideas ever since.

Anyone can tap into the creative mindset and begin using the creative talents that God has given them. In fact, part of our life's purpose is to use and multiply our creative talents, doing as much good as we can while here on Earth.

If I didn't apply what I teach in this book, I wouldn't be living my life's purpose, using my God-given talents to create and share my experiences with others. I'd still be dreaming about singing, writing, and performing, not living my life as a singer and author. You may be thinking, "I'm not creative. I don't have a talent." Trust me, you are and you do, you just haven't discovered how to tap into that creative vein. This program will help you unleash your creativity, find your talent, and become creatively successful.

When I use the word "successful," I'm not referring to financial success. I'm referring to something far greater—knowledge, because knowledge unlocks creativity, which leads to success in all areas of your life. In the Bible, King Solomon knew that knowledge was the greatest wealth a man could possess. Through knowledge, he attained success beyond belief, including material wealth. Through knowledge you can do the same, becoming mentally, physically, spiritually, and, of course, financially successful, and experiencing a deeper sense of accomplishment.

For those who are wondering if this is another law of attraction program, think of it more as a "law of action" program. If you're ready for action, ready to discover the true creative nature within you, and ready to work toward creating what you envision, all to experience the fruits of your creative success, read on.

As I tapped into my creative mindset, I developed a passion for working toward my goals, which led to the realization that creativity enforces your motivational success drive. The success drive is what every successful person and genius experiences. We all have the ability to think like a successful genius, but most of us leave the door to creativity and positive motivation closed. Once you open this door to the floodgates of creativity, you'll automatically flip your motivational switch to the ON position. You will become driven beyond imagination, as your mind begins releasing countless ideas and creative possibilities.

In my quest to unlock this door, I researched numerous self-help books and programs. Most methods were too intricate and had too many steps, and I quickly lost interest. Other programs bored me, such as the book that said, "Wish it and you're done."

So I decided to create my own approach, one that was easy to do, that would keep my interest. I related the creative mindset concepts to something that I used every day—the computer. After all, we're each our own computer. Let me explain:

I'm on my computer hours every day, writing books, conducting online voice lessons over Skype, answering questions on message boards, and promoting through social networking sites. The Internet is also my link to endless information as I gather data for the books I write. The Internet has quickly become an important tool for collecting data that we can use to excel.

Once we've retrieved data from the World Wide Web, where do we store this information? Besides our computer's hard drive, we store it in our mind computer. Each of us has a built-in computer unmatched by any other. It's called the "brain." Your brain allows you to think, feel, see, touch, taste, and smell ... and store terabytes of data. It's also connected to your subconscious mind, which is the invisible self that keeps the heart pumping, body breathing, wounds healing, etc.

To further elaborate, the subconscious mind is connected to the largest information resource available, or what I've already referred to as the creative mindset. The creative mindset is the subconscious on steroids. It is our connection to unlimited amounts of information and creativity; it is the Universal Wide Web. How would you like to surf www.tonsofgreatideas.com?

The creative mindset is what inspires the author to write an amazing novel, aids the mathematician in solving a complicated equation, moves the artist to write a beautiful piece of music, provides a person with the perfect solution to their problem in the blink of an eye. The creative mindset is your digital data bank of the knowledge you learn and the knowledge waiting to be discovered.

The Mindset program will teach you how to use your mind like a computer to access that digital data bank. It will teach you to install new mental software programs into your subconscious to think more like a genius, strive harder, and work smarter. Once you've installed new programs, you'll run them every day to keep the creative floodgates open and the motivational switch flipped to the ON position.

What can you achieve by applying the Mindset program? You can write new songs, author books, overcome stage fright, discipline your mind to achieve better school grades, relieve mental and physical stress, eliminate writer's block, break bad habits, and more.

These techniques work! It doesn't matter whether you're an artist, writer, inventor, business owner, musician, stay-at-home mom, or aspiring dreamer, you CAN unlock your creative mindset.

Are you ready to unlock your creative mindset and discover what talents you possess? If you said YES to both questions, get ready to unleash the creative floodgates. But before we jump into the mindset program, let's learn about your mental computer.

Getting To Know Your Super Computer

YOU OWN THE WORLD'S most intricate computer—your brain—which consists of the conscious and subconscious. Your computer is so amazing that it can help you create beautiful works of art, solve complex mathematical equations, and mentally influence the outcome of most situations.

Think of your brain as your central processing unit that deals with everyday conscious activities. The brain is divided into two halves. The right half of the brain, also referred to as the visual side, focuses on colors, shapes, and music, and it controls the left side of your body. Daydreamers are considered right-brained. If you're left-handed, be sure to tell all your right-handed friends that you're the only one in your right mind. I know that's an old joke. I just accessed it from my mind computer.

Right-brained people are said to be great poets, musicians, writers, and artists. Leonardo Da Vinci was probably right-brained, as was Albert Einstein. It might seem odd to think of Einstein as right-brained, but he did poorly in school, most likely because he was too busy daydreaming.

The left half of the brain, or the analytical side, controls the right side of your body and is said to be the control center for deep thinking, such as solving mathematical equations. Left-brained people are said to make good lawyers, politicians, mathematicians, and bankers.

One more thought: Einstein was considered right-brained, yet he was a physicist (left-brain function). This just goes to show that we are both left- and right-brained, but most of us typically develop one side more than the other. This doesn't mean that we can't be equally gifted in math and music or art and politics. In fact, your goal should be to balance both sides of your brain in order to access your unlimited creative potential. You CAN be a rock star and a rocket scientist, aka "rocket star scientist," but only if you have the drive and desire.

Just as one computer differs from another, so do our mind computers. Your desktop computer may be ten years old (aka the Stone Age) and used for bookkeeping only, while your new laptop is running a quadcore processor with 8 gigs of RAM, strictly for recording music.

Our mind computers come in different types, running at different speeds, but we're always upgrading them, just as we can upgrade our desktop and laptop computers. We cannot, however, upgrade our mind computers by shoving a memory stick in our ear. Ouch! We upgrade through experiencing life. As we gain new knowledge, we evolve as individuals and are mentally upgraded.

As you study a subject such as algebra or physics, you add knowledge to your mental hard drive, which automatically upgrades your processing speed. The more you draw cartoons or play music, the more skilled you become at those tasks, because you are upgrading your mind computer.

Anyone can tap into new forms of genius through upgrading. Maybe you feel that you haven't unlocked the genius within yet. Not to worry; we all have the ability to achieve and do great things, but it takes time and focus to upgrade to the point where you're ready for more success. How much success is determined by which programs we decide to install.

BRAIN FACTS
Here are a few interesting facts about our mind computer:

- The brain is the most complex machine ever! No computer built by man even comes close!

- No man-made computer can calculate the amount of bytes per second that our mind is capable of handling!

- It weighs only about three pounds by the time you reach adulthood. That's pretty light for an amazing machine!

- It has about one hundred billion nerve cells. That's a lot of nerve!

- It uses twenty percent of the body's oxygen and blood supply. That's a lot of air!

- We've only tapped a few percent of its mental possibilities. Imagine what we could accomplish with only a few more!
- The brain, heart, and gut connect our conscious mind to our subconscious. Combining the power of all three is the secret to tapping into your creative success!

By combining the power of brain, heart, and gut, we can utilize the power of both our mind and our emotions to ignite the creativity within, because emotion is pure, creative fuel. To prove it, think of a memory from your past when you were extremely upset. Can you recall the heartache you experienced when your favorite pet died or the sadness from losing your first love? Do you remember that knot in your stomach, lump in your throat, or aching in your heart from the pain of these memories?

Your emotions act like file extensions, so that you can easily search for any memory, just like using the search function on your desktop. Whenever you were nervous, excited, scared, mad, or extremely happy and felt that sensation in the throat, heart, or gut, your subconscious mind instantly attached that emotion to the experience, forever linking it to the memory. Your mind can recall all of your emotional memories in great detail, which is an invaluable tool, as you'll soon discover.

YOUR HARD DRIVE

The subconscious mind functions as your mental hard drive and is the storehouse for all of your past memories, emotions, and a life's worth of accumulated knowledge. Luckily for us, the storage space is unlimited. It's where musicians store countless songs, an actor stores the lines of a play, a linguist stores multiple languages.

Your unlimited hard drive is always increasing. When you were an infant you started out with a basic hard drive and immediately began adding more data through your new experiences.

I can remember purchasing my first computer. The salesman told me it had a 4.3-gigabyte hard drive and that I would *never* use that much storage space. Six months later, I needed more storage. I spent a hundred bucks for a 10-gigabyte hard drive. I thought that was a deal, only to watch the price soon drop as the 10-gig was replaced by a 20-gig, 40-gig, 60, 80, 100 ...

Since our mental hard drives have unlimited space, you'll never need to delete old memories. It doesn't mean all those memories are immediately available for instant recall. When we quit running a program, such as algebra, or we quit replaying an old memory in our mind, such as a camping trip with our grandparents, the mind will file that program or memory way in the back, and it can be recalled at a later date if needed. File organization is automatically performed by the subconscious mind so that we don't have to spend countless hours organizing those mental files. This automatic subconscious file organization depends on two factors:

1. **The amount of time spent using the program.** If you use your program every day, it will be one of your top files. However, if you quit using your program, it will soon be archived.
2. **The amount of emotion attached to a memory.** Strong emotional memories are stored in the very front of your mental file system; memories with lesser emotional ties are stored toward the back. Files can also be moved to

the very back once the emotion, such as the pain from a breakup, begins to fade away.

I recall being very adept at trigonometry because I enjoyed it. It was one of the "programs" I could run efficiently. I became a trigonometry whiz, which upgraded my CPU. I haven't used that program for years, so it's been stored in the back of my mental hard drive. If I needed to use trigonometry today, I would have to relearn a few equations, but I know that once I began brushing up on my math skills, I would begin pulling those old files from the back folders of my mind.

How do you pull old files? It's like riding a bicycle; you get back on. If it's trigonometry, you review your math skills. If it's a memory of your childhood pet, you can access that old memory by spending time recalling details about your pet, looking at old photos, watching videos, etc. Mental, physical, and visual stimulation is the key to accessing old files.

Once you've recalled an older memory or program, you can only keep it in the front of your hard drive through repetitively recalling the memory or by repeatedly using the program. Repetition makes you better at everything you do. The more you play basketball, the better you become; the more you cook, the better chef you'll be; the more you write, the easier the words will flow.

Use the Mindset program regularly, and you'll find that it's much easier to stay focused, motivated, and positive, which helps you accomplish your goals and bring more success into your life. That's the goal, right? Now back to your hard drive.

I have lots of great childhood memories that I'll remember for my entire life. That's because of the emotions attached to them. It's easier to access memories that have strong emotional significance, especially when tied to any of the five senses—hearing, sight, touch, smell, and taste. This is why I can recall the time I slipped on a pile of dog poop (smell) and cracked my head (pain) at the age of five. It isn't my most favorite childhood memory, but you can understand why I can remember it vividly.

Now it's your turn. What is the earliest childhood memory you can recall? Replay that memory three times in a row like watching a short video clip on YouTube. You'll notice that every time you replayed the memory, you developed a more detailed view of the past. Repetition makes the mind grow stronger. Congratulations, you have just successfully accessed a file from your hard drive.

Not all files are this easy to recall. For instance, if you have a great meal at a restaurant with three of your best friends from college and then don't eat there for six months, I bet you can easily recall what a great time you had and how great the food tasted that night. That's because it's stored in the front of your hard drive, a result of all the mental and emotional stimulation. However, if you decide to eat the same meal at that same restaurant day after day for six months, you won't be able to recall every occasion, even though you've stored those memories.

Why is this so? Because you've dulled the experience. Yes, you'll definitely remember what the food tastes like, but there are few if any emotional ties for each individual day. The only occasions you'll be able to recall easily will be those that do have some emotional impact, like the waiter slipping on a big wet spot on the floor and getting food all over his shirt, which made you laugh. Don't worry; no waiters were harmed in the making of this visual.

On the flip side, the subconscious could automatically store an extremely painful memory in the back of your mind because the emotional connection is too intense to handle. Our mind considers it a potential danger to our computer and views the memory as a virus. If the subconscious feels too much pain associated with a memory, it may hide the file. These files are never lost or deleted but are buried in our hard drive, waiting to be dealt with when their owner is ready. Remember, our hard drive saves every thought we've ever had.

Enough of the emotional stuff. Let's get back to the subject of upgrading our computer. I've upgraded my desktop computer several times. I've added more memory and installed bigger hard drives to speed it up and expand the space so I could add more files and programs.

With an actual computer, you can add another stick of memory to make the processing speed faster and swap out a hard drive for a larger one with more storage space. You should recall that we upgrade our mind computer through increasing our knowledge by learning new subjects, solving complex mathematical equations, and creating mental stimulation through visualization, music, art, etc.

To move toward greater success, the first goal is to begin upgrading your mind by surrounding yourself with projects that relate to your talent. If your passion is to become a dancer or a dance instructor, surround yourself with dance-related activities. If your passion is to become a writer, you must begin writing every single day. Don't get stressed, we'll address this soon enough. For now, read on.

YOUR AUDIO/VIDEO SYSTEM

Now that I've covered your CPU and hard drive, I'd like to introduce you to your internal audio/video system. Close your eyes and look at the blank screen on the inside of your eyelids. On that blank screen, visualize the ocean moving back and forth onto a beach. Listen to the sound of the waves crashing. Feel the sand between your toes as the water rushes over your feet. Take a deep breath to smell and taste the salty air.

We have an amazing ability to re-create memories. We can visualize pictures and reconstruct sounds, smells, tastes, feelings, and emotions with great accuracy. We re-create these memories by accessing our mental hard drive to see, hear, taste, touch, smell, and experience vivid mental movies. You *are* the perfect audio and video entertainment system, complete with internal surround sound!

SETTING UP YOUR MONITOR

Your monitor is a cathedral of infinite space inside your head that exists right behind your closed eyes. It's adjustable to any size screen, from a small two-inch square to the size of a drive-in movie theater, viewable in black and white or full color.

My mind monitor is HUGE. I remember in my youth going to the movies, sitting in the very front row. The screen was so close that I had to look up to watch the movie. I felt like I was part of the film. That's how I visualize as well.

Your mental monitor can play reruns of past memories, show you mental pictures that can help solve your problems, or be used to make your own movies to program your subconscious mind to achieve your personal goals. Take a moment to rerun a memory on your monitor. When you've finished, we'll talk about your Internet connection.

The Ultimate Internet Experience

While the subconscious is your storehouse for all your personal experiences, the creative mindset is the storehouse for those flashes of creative genius you'll soon be experiencing. It's your ultimate Internet connection, always on and accessible.

Have you ever experienced one of those "eureka moments" when you desperately needed the solution to a problem, such as finishing the lyrics for a new song, and suddenly the answer seemed to pop suddenly into your consciousness? That's the creative mindset at work.

The creative mindset is the knowledge bank or source of creativity that Tesla and Edison tapped into when they created hundreds of inventions. It is the source of Mozart's musical genius, Picasso's artistic inspiration, and Martin Luther King's insights for his life-changing "I Have a Dream" speech.

Think of it like this: An artist requires many tools to create a masterpiece, including paint, brushes, pastels, oils, and a canvas. But even with all the necessary physical tools, the artist cannot create a masterpiece unless he or she can withdraw knowledge and inspiration from the creative mindset. Without the creative materials of the mind, the painting would never come to life.

We all have the ability to access this vast bank of information. For this reason, two people on opposite sides of the world can tap into the same idea for the same invention at the same time. If you've got an idea for a new invention, you had better get it out there before someone in Australia—or Brazil, India, Norway, or Mozambique—beats you to it!

Whether you want to use the Mindset program to tap into your artistic creativity, write a hit song, discover your true hidden talent, or develop the unbridled motivation to tackle and accomplish any goal, you can do it. It will work equally well for any and all aspirations you have.

I believe you now have an understanding of your mind computer and the creative mindset, so let's begin the Mindset program.

Keeping A Journal

THE FIRST STEP in the Mindset program requires that you start a journal. But this journal is special. You'll write down answers to five specific questions, purposely chosen to stimulate your creative side in a way that guides you toward success. The act of writing will not only help you unleash your creative mindset but also help you harness it.

Writing is by far the perfect tool for stimulating your creative mindset, because it sends messages to the subconscious mind and also prompts messages *from* the subconscious mind. Whatever questions you ask the subconscious, it will work relentlessly to provide an answer.

Once the subconscious mind has its orders, it will begin sending messages to your conscious mind to give you answers and guide you toward solving the problem you've asked about. Have you ever noticed how whenever you become interested in a subject, for example, playing guitar, that all of a sudden you begin to see guitars everywhere you look? You see television commercials for a music store full of guitars, you see someone playing guitar on a street corner, you get an email from someone who sells a guitar course, you stumble onto a website for new guitarists. This is happening because your subconscious is focused on answering your questions by achieving a solution. The subconscious pays attention to everything that your conscious mind fails to notice.

From this day forward, you should keep a journal with you at all times. As you ask the five questions, you will begin receiving random flashes of thought focused around them. If you don't keep track of these random thoughts in your journal, you risk of losing great ideas.

Keep your journal with you always—in the car, at your workplace, at a restaurant, in the bathroom, beside your bed, wherever you are.

Your creative mindset can spark new ideas and send you messages at any time of day or night, including when you're asleep, so you must always be prepared to capture your ideas on paper. Whenever an answer comes to you, write it down as soon as you can and as fast as you can before that thought evaporates.

My sixth-grade English teacher required our class to keep a journal for the entire year. Through that experience, I found a passion for writing. Ever since then, I've jotted down my daily thoughts as fast as they came to me. Over the years, I've kept journals on multiple subjects, including electronics, music theory, diet and health, marketing, and singing, to name just five of them.

You'll find that the more you write in your journal, the more your mind comes alive with ideas. However, there are times when writing in a journal doesn't work, such as when you're driving a car or when you need to sing a melody line. A digital audio recorder is your best friend during those times, because you can record on the fly and then transcribe your thoughts into your journal later in the day. You can also use your cell phone to record, if it offers recording and notepad capabilities.

You never know when that flash of genius will burst into your consciousness, so always have the means to capture your ideas on paper or audio.

Now that you're ready to start a journal, let's discuss the best way to use it. The Mindset program is based on the Mind/Body process (which we'll discuss later), along with the following five questions that you will be required to answer daily in your journal:

- *WHAT WILL I DO TODAY TO BETTER MYSELF?*

- *WHAT AM I IN THE PROCESS OF DOING?*

- *DO I HAVE ANY NEW IDEAS?*

- *WHAT AM I THANKFUL FOR?*

- *WHAT DID I DO TODAY TO BETTER MYSELF?*

These five questions stimulate the creative mindset and boost your creative thinking skills. To keep the creative juices flowing, it's important to ask all five questions every day. Once you've asked a question, do not force an answer; you must *allow* the answers to come to you. Forcing or rushing an answer is like turning an oven two hundred degrees too high to bake a cake in less time than the recipe calls for. You'll get a "cake," but you won't want to serve it to guests. A forced answer won't serve your needs, because it didn't come from your creative mindset.

Fortunately, the questions "What will I do today to better myself" and "What did I do today to better myself?" will keep your subconscious and conscious minds both working toward achieving your goals. You won't have spare time to fabricate an answer, because these two questions create what I call *direction* and *reflection*.

"What will I do today to better myself?" creates a sense of direction, which will keep your motivational switch flipped to the ON position throughout the day, thus pumping the creative mindset for new information. "What did I do today to better myself?" prompts you to reflect on your accomplishments throughout the day, which causes you to "sleep on" those accomplishments. You'll wake up the next morning even more driven toward reaching your goals. Direction and reflection boost your motivational drive and your positive attitude.

To be successful, you must always feel as if you are experiencing success as a way of life. A negative attitude will weaken your ability to access the creative mindset. By staying positive, you'll become a motivational machine geared toward achieving your goals. You have a choice to be positive or negative every day. Choose wisely.

The three remaining questions will come to you at random times throughout your day, whenever a situation occurs that applies to a specific question. An example would be coming up with that elusive chorus to a song you've been writing for months. You could immediately ask, "What am I thankful for? I am thankful the melody finally came to me so I can finish this great song!"

Now it's time to format your journal, or set it up for writing. The two best formats are:

A. Write one question at the top of each page for five pages.
B. Spread out the five questions equally on a single page, allowing room below each question for your answers.

It doesn't matter how you format your journal, but don't delay. In case you've forgotten, the five questions are:

WHAT WILL I DO TODAY TO BETTER MYSELF?
WHAT AM I IN THE PROCESS OF DOING?
DO I HAVE ANY NEW IDEAS?
WHAT AM I THANKFUL FOR?
WHAT DID I DO TODAY TO BETTER MYSELF?

As you begin writing in your journal, make sure to date each section to maintain a record of your thoughts. For the single-page layout, write the date beside each set of daily answers. For the one-question-per-page layout, date the top corner of each page. Dates provide an accurate history when you look through your diary to review past answers. When reviewing, you'll discover that your answers interlace between questions. For example, on one date you might have been *thankful* for a new idea about a song you were *in the process* of writing. For now, don't worry about remembering the five questions, because we'll discuss each question as we proceed through the book. Before we begin writing, we must master the Mind/Body process, which takes us to the next chapter.

The Mind/Body Process

THE MIND/BODY PROCESS was created to relieve the physical and mental stress that impedes our ability to access the creative mindset. Daily life can lead to a negative attitude and physical and mental exhaustion, which affects our ability to stay positive and motivated.

The Mind/Body process improves focus, relieves physical and mental stress, flips the motivation switch to ON, and opens the door to your creativity so that you can step inside your "creativity bank" and make a withdrawal.

The Mind/Body process consists of several steps, starting by praying to God. Personally for me, without acknowledging and thanking God, my success rate rapidly plummets, therefore I always pray. Following prayer, we will perform a simple breathing exercise that increases oxygen levels, which warms up the mind and body. Then we'll let go of all physical stress in the muscles to allow the body to function more efficiently. After releasing muscular tension, we'll calm the mind for mental clarity and balance the left brain/right brain to stabilize our thought process. We'll end the Mind/Body process by clearing out mental clutter and installing creativity programs. Let's get started.

DISCLAIMER: Before we start the Mind/Body process, I want to state that the entire Mindset program is not intended to prescribe, treat, prevent, or diagnose any physical or mental illness. Please consult your physician before performing any of the exercises in this book.

STEP I: PRAYER

As you already know, the first step in the process is prayer. Think of prayer as the catalyst that ignites your creativity. My mother taught me to pray at a very young age, and I have been praying ever since. She explained that everything comes from God. God guides us, protects us, provides for us, and is present in everything we see and feel, from the air we breathe to the stones we skip across a lake. Prayer lets us know we're never alone. Because of prayer, I've never felt alone. I pray every morning, throughout the day, and before I go to bed. Why is prayer so important? Remember how I said that God is both the owner and manager of the bank of knowledge? You cannot make a withdrawal without approval from the manager of the bank. Prayer is a way to quit focusing on yourself and focus on God. Praying to God appeases the manager. If you don't pray, the manager will deny the loan.

Everything we have, everything we see, everything we know is because of God. All the ideas we receive through our creative mindset come from God. There is no quicker way to close the door on creativity than to deny acknowledgement, gratitude, and praise to God.

Back to Step I. The first thing I do when I wake is stretch, smile, and say, "This is going to be a great day!" When you first wake up, say something positive as you smile, because you never want to start your day in a bad mood. You can repeat my phrase or make up one of your own. Once you've set a positive thought into your mind, it's time to pray.

When I pray, I begin as if I am speaking to my best friend, telling God how thankful I am that He protects and provides for me, and I acknowledge my love for Him. I pray from my heart as if I'm having a one-on-one conversation. I also recite specific prayers that are special to me, such as the Lord's Prayer, the Prayer of Jabez, and the Ana B'Koach, which is also known as the Miracle Prayer or Genesis Prayer. (Books that refer to these prayers are listed in the Appendix.) I sometimes add other prayers, but I always pray from the heart.

Prayer for me isn't about myself, it's more about God. However, I've recited specific prayers and will sometimes pray for health, wealth, and success. If I'm focused on accomplishing a certain goal, and if it's a goal by God's will, I "pray it in the now," asking that it has already come to pass and giving thanks for the successful outcome. Before I became a vocal coach, I used to pray "Thank you, Lord, for blessing my vocal coaching career."

I finish by praying for others, thanking God for the many blessings I've received, and asking for guidance throughout the day and forgiveness for my many errors.

Once I have finished my prayers, I end with "In Jesus name, Amen." You don't have to pray exactly as I do, as I know my way stems from my Christian nature. You should find your own way to speak to God, but make sure you speak to God!

How truly powerful is prayer? After I prayed to God, asking if I should continue performing on television, within twenty-four hours, I got booked for my first television show in two years. Responses for television shows and vocal workshops in Japan, Bahrain, Australia, China, Europe, and the United States followed shortly thereafter. This proves that God listens to us and answers our prayers.

People need the power of prayer. We tend to pray only when we are in deep trouble or when things are going really well, but when we are cruising along with no excitement in our lives, we tend to forget about our connection to God. Prayer changes lives, so make prayer a part of your life. Put this book down and pray for a moment. Once you've finished praying, we'll get oxygenated.

Note: This system will work without prayer, but not as effective without that catalyst. It is the initial spark that guides you and releases your creativity. Don't skip this step to speed things up. It will only slam on the brakes.

STEP II: OXYGEN BOOSTING
Step II of the Mind/Body process is designed to distribute oxygen to the body to energize brain cells and other cells. Remember, the brain

uses twenty percent of our oxygen supply, so we're going to pump and prime that twenty percent to feed our supercomputer for maximum efficiency.

This exercise, which I call the "Extreme Breathing Exercise," increases oxygen in the bloodstream, which is said to boost physical performance, immune defense, and metabolism. The following steps break down the exercise:

1.) While lying flat on your back, take a deep, slow breath, allowing the belly to expand like a balloon, then exhale, allowing the belly to relax and drop back down. This is how babies breathe:

   Inhale = belly up
   Exhale = belly down

   Note: For more information on breathing techniques and exercises, please refer to *The Ultimate Breathing Workout* book and *Beyond the Ultimate Breathing Workout* video at venderapublishing.com.

2.) With your mouth closed, inhale through the nose for a count of four, and then open and exhale through the mouth for a count of four. Allow the stomach to rise high and drop low. Repeat this step four times.
3.) With your mouth closed, inhale through the nose for a count of two, and then open and exhale through the mouth for a count of two. Repeat this step eight times.
4.) Next, inhale through an open mouth for a count of one, and then exhale though the mouth for a count of one. Repeat this step sixteen times.
5.) Next, with mouth open, pant thirty-two times.
6.) Repeat the process in reverse, beginning by inhaling through your mouth for a count of one and exhaling though

the mouth for a count of one. Repeat this step sixteen times.

7.) Next, with mouth closed, inhale through the nose for a count of two, and then exhale through the mouth for a count of two. Repeat this step eight times.

8.) Last, with mouth closed, inhale through the nose for a count of four, and then open and exhale through the mouth for a count of four. Allow your stomach to rise high and drop low. Repeat this step four times.

Inhale as deeply and exhale as completely as you can during this exercise. Increasing oxygen to the bloodstream may make you feel relaxed and rejuvenated, warm and tingly, or even a bit light-headed. Expelling all the air from your lungs will help to release stagnant air (carbon dioxide) from your lungs. This might give you bad breath because of the release of toxins. You can brush your teeth or take a breath mint. Increasing oxygen intake can produce astounding health-related benefits. It can jumpstart your metabolism, boost your fat-burning capabilities, strengthen your immune system, stimulate your mind, and energize your body. Now that you're full of air, let's move on to the next step.

STEP III: ENERGIZING THE BODY

Step III will release physical tension and energize your muscles. Have you ever experienced the tingling sensation of your foot falling asleep? Do you remember how your foot felt as if it were vibrating? For this step, we will visualize that same sensation through the body. While lying on your bed (or sitting in a chair) follow these instructions:

1.) Tense your left foot as hard as you can, and then relax it. Allow the tingling sensation to wash over all of your toes and cover the entire top of the foot, heel, arch, and sole until your entire left foot is completely covered with the tingling sensation. Switch to the right foot. Tense and relax the right foot and allow the tingling sensation to work its way through your toes, sole, heel, and arch, covering the entire right foot.

Note: We'll begin alternating from left side to right, all the way up your body. Once you've created this tingling sensation in any part of your body, you must continue to visualize feeling the vibration.

2.) Next, tense and relax your left calf, and then immediately allow the tingling sensation to work from the foot, up the lower leg, to the kneecap. Remember that any part of the body that you have relaxed should remain tingling. Switch to your right leg, tense and release the calf, and then allow the energy to spread and cover the lower right leg up to the right kneecap.

3.) You should now feel as if you have been immersed in this tingling sensation all the way up to above your kneecaps. If any muscle feels tight, simply visualize the muscle relaxing as you perform these steps. If you experience any knots in your muscles, visualize each knot shrinking until it is completely gone.

4.) Tense and relax the left thigh, allowing the tingling sensation to float up and cover the thigh completely to the socket of the pelvic bone. Imagine that this tingling sensation is a bath of energy that is releasing stress, healing old wounds, rebuilding tissue, and removing disease and infection. Close your eyes, and on your mind monitor, picture the tingling sensation as a pulsating strobe light covering every part of your body that's resonating. Allow the strobe light to spread throughout the body as the vibration spreads. Repeat the process for the right thigh.

5.) Tense and relax the gluteus muscles and the genitals, allowing the tingling sensation to envelop the entire body up to your hipbones.

6.) Tense and relax your abdominal and back muscles. Allow the tingling sensation to cover the entire area, front and back, up to your lower ribs. Visualize being submerged in a hot spring as the tingling sensation moves up around your body. Feel the warmth of the hot spring healing your aches and pains.

7.) Moving up from the stomach, tense and release the ribs, chest, and shoulders, allowing the energy to cover the entire body from the shoulders down, with the exception of the arms.

8.) Begin tensing and relaxing the left bicep and tricep muscles, allowing the energy to flow down into and covering the upper left arm, producing the same tingling sensation. Repeat the process for the upper right arm.

9.) Tense and relax your left forearm by curling your fist, with the palm toward your inner forearm. Allow the tingling sensation of the energy to flow downward, covering your left forearm. Repeat the process with the right forearm.

10.) Squeeze your left hand into a tight fist, and then open your hand up wide, wiggling your fingers. Feel the tingling sensation flow from your forearm down into your hand, covering the entire hand and flowing out the ends of your fingertips. Visualize strobe lights flowing out of each fingertip, releasing any stress from the body. Repeat for the right hand.

11.) Tense and squeeze your neck, jaw, and face tightly, and then relax your neck and facial muscles. Allow the resonant sensation to start working up your neck, relieving tension in your neck and throat and continuing upward to cover your chin and jaw. Stretch your jaw open wide to relieve all tension. Feel your nose and ears tingling. Feel the sensation covering the back of your head. Allow any strain to leave your eyes. Feel as if the energy is cleansing and opening your ears, eyes, sinuses, and hair follicles, rebuilding and restoring sight, sound, smell, and hair growth. Continue until you feel the top of your head tingling. At this point, you should feel as if you are completely submerged in the hot spring.

12.) Once you've reached the state of total submersion, allow that tingling connection to flow upwards from the top of your skull to your creative mindset. If it helps, you can visualize a laser shooting straight up into the sky as if it's a direct line connecting to the creative mindset, the ultimate ISP. I pretend the laser is like a telephone line reaching out to God. This is a perfect time for prayer. You can never pray too much.

13.) Now that the ISP is connected, visualize a giant sparkler inside your body from head to toe. Allow the sparkler to light at the top of your head and burn its way down from head to toe, burning up any remaining stress. Allow this final visual cleansing make you feel as if you're removing ALL stagnant energy from your body. In reality, we're all made up of tiny energetic particles that become negatively affected by stress. So visualize this sparkler as a means to remove the rest of your stress.

For those of you who think this is a bit far-fetched for your personal beliefs, you should know that these basic visualizations help to open up your creativity by expanding your imagination, so just go with it. Step outside the box. Now it's time to access our hard drive.

STEP IV: ACCESSING YOUR HARD DRIVE

Step IV will allow you to access your hard drive in order to organize old files and install new programs. We'll begin by focusing on the blank screen on the front of our eyelids. Using your mind monitor, you'll count backwards from the number 7 to the number 1 as you visualize a specific color in a specific order.

Close your eyes and visualize the number **7** on your monitor. Visualize drawing a **7** on the blank space of your eyelids. Now visualize a **RED 7**. Coloring each number is very important! Once you can see the colored number on your monitor, repeat the same process for each number as follows: Visualize an **ORANGE 6**. After you have held this vision for a few moments, visualize a **YELLOW 5**. When you're ready, visualize a **GREEN 4**. After a few moments, visualize a **BLUE 3**. Next, visualize an **INDIGO 2**. Last, visualize a **VIOLET 1**.

As you visualize each colored number on your monitor, allow it to gradually become smaller. Do NOT visualize the words; visualize only colored numbers. You must visualize the number in its color, allowing each one to become smaller and smaller on your monitor. Please flip to the back cover of this book right now for a visual reference to the shrinking colored numbers.

This visualization helps bring the left brain/right brain into balance. Counting stimulates your analytical (left) brain, while visualizing color stimulates the artistic (right) brain. Counting backwards from seven to one also allows your mind to slip deeper and deeper into a trancelike state, reaching a mental point that will soon allow you to access files stored in your mental hard drive.

Once you have finished counting backwards, we must defragment and clean up our mental disk space before file searching.

STEP V: DEFRAGMENTING YOUR HARD DRIVE

Surfing the net and downloading files builds up a lot of junk on a hard drive, which affects the computer's speed and efficiency. The same can happen with the mind. We get bogged down with mental junk every day because our mind races with random thoughts, like the ticker running at the bottom of the television screen when the news is on. In Step V, we'll defragment our computer to clean up our files.

Before beginning this step, you'll need a timer. I use a timer app on my iPhone. (Soon there will be an Mindset app with a diary and timer, because I am "in the process" of developing one.) Make sure to get a timer that doesn't make noise during countdown. It should be quiet until the four-minute alarm sounds. Using a timer prevents you from repeatedly looking at the clock every few seconds, a deadly distraction. Full focus is required!

Set your timer, close your eyes, and begin to focus on inhaling through your nose and exhaling through your mouth. Place the tips of the index, middle, and ring fingers of each hand on your temples. Use the tips of your fingers to feel for a pulse on each temple. Once you've placed the fingers of your left hand on your left temple, and the fingers of your right hand on your right temple, you may have to move your fingers around until you find each pulse.

Once you can feel the pulse, imagine a blank screen on your mind monitor. Your goal is to think of absolutely nothing except the pulse against your fingertips while you stare at the blank screen. As random thoughts pop into your head (and they will), you must delete them. Wandering thoughts are like pop-ups on the Internet. When a thought appears, simply visualize deleting that thought (pop-up) by clicking an imaginary **X** on your mental screen. When images such as random light patterns float onto your monitor, just let them float right off the screen. Do not try to follow them with your eyes, or they will become trapped on the screen and tempt you to follow them around as they swim up and down or side to side across the backs of your eyelids.

Continue to focus on the rhythm of your pulse against your fingertips, which will help eliminate random thoughts, especially if you breathe with the rhythm of your pulse. Inhale for four pulses and exhale for four pulses. Continue breathing to the rhythm while deleting any thoughts that intrude. Once the timer goes off, you're finished defragmenting your hard drive.

You may feel happier, lighter, less stressed, and even more confident. That's the goal. Always start your day in a great mood.

Why would you want to start your day in a bad mood? Like attracts like, so don't promote negativity.

Flooding your body with oxygen, letting go of physical stress, energizing your muscles, and allowing your mind to clear away mental junk promotes a healthier body and a healthier state of mind. If you truly want to accomplish your goals, you should start with the Mind/Body process.

Some of you might be saying, "I feel great now, but what about accomplishing my goals or unleashing my creative mindset?" Your answer awaits you in the last step.

STEP VI: INSTALLING NEW PROGRAMS (OPTIONAL)

Step VI of the Mind/Body process is the key to installing new "thought" programs onto the mental hard drive. Think of a program as new mental software containing all the correct thoughts needed to bring artistic creativity and motivation into your life in order to achieve any goal successfully.

Step VI doesn't need to be performed every day. Use it only when you feel you need to install a brand-new program. Once you've installed that program, you don't need to install it again, unless you've lost focus. It's like installing a new program on your desktop computer; you install it only once, unless you accidentally delete it. When upgrading to a newer version, we only install the upgrade. To reiterate, perform this step only once, unless you've lost your focus or you want to upgrade that program to include new thoughts.

What can you install? Any creative goal you have your heart set on, as long as it does not cause harm or negatively affect another person. When installing new programs, every thought connects to the creative mindset to guide you toward the success of that program, giving you the motivational drive needed to reach your financial, physical, emotional, and spiritual goals.

Time for an exercise: Grab a pen and some paper and make a list of seven goals you'd like to accomplish. Though I'm not keen on using the Mindset program for material possessions, as I feel you'll proceed down that avenue through your own creative efforts, you can still add a few material objects you'd like to obtain. After all, Mindset is simply a way to program your mind to bypass procrastination and focus on creatively reaching your goals. In that respect, there is nothing wrong with material possessions, because the creative mindset works toward obtaining the material possessions by using your creativity in a positive manner for the betterment of all. Your creative outcome may help you obtain material things, but the end result of your creativity will help others as well. For this exercise, it doesn't matter how large or how small the goal or material object, just write down the first thing that comes to mind. Here's an example list:

- A ten percent pay increase
- Easel, brushes, and paint set
- An idea for a new fiction book
- To attend night classes for a degree
- A better relationship with your spouse
- A great, original song idea
- The knowledge to build your own website

Each entry represents one new program that can be installed. Once you have a list, you can install one per day over the next seven days. Here's how to install your first program.

Let's pretend that you want to install a program for that great song. Reset your timer, place your fingertips on your temples, and begin viewing the program on your monitor, as if you were watching a movie. Involve all five senses and visualize all the positive emotions you'd experience as you were writing that song. Live the scene in your mind in great detail, including the smile on your face as you write it and the cheers of your fans as you perform the song live. If you can see and feel your goal, you can accomplish it! But, in order to be successful, you have to experience every sense and emotion to make it real; you have to feel as if it has already been accomplished.

THE FOUR-MINUTE MIRACLE

I remember reading an article many years ago about how some meditation teachers believe that if you can concentrate on one goal for four straight minutes, without interruption, you will accomplish that goal. I believe this, so it's no coincidence that we defragment and program our mind for four minutes each.

Are you ready for the Mindset challenge? Do you *really* want to develop the motivation required to achieve your goals? Do you *really* want to tap into your creative genius and become a huge success? Do you *really* think you can you concentrate on one program for four minutes without interruption?" If you answered "YES" to all three questions, get ready to be transformed into a success machine!

The very first time I installed a new program, I internally chanted, "I am in the process of becoming a successful vocal coach." I silently repeated this affirmation over and over in my mind as I felt the rhythm of my pulse. On my mental monitor, I visualized all that's involved in becoming a professional vocal coach. I visualized my website, my first book, and giving voice lessons. I used all five senses, and I felt the excitement of thousands of singers as their voices improved.

In hindsight, my first program installation was too complex. I should have installed one program at a time over a period of three days, one for vocal coach, one for website development, and one for writing a book, but I was learning how to make this system work. When installing your first program, I suggest narrowing your goal down to one clearly understood program. Although I overloaded my mental hard drive by installing three programs at once, I did accomplish all three goals, but it would have been much smarter to install one program at a time.

After I installed my first program, I *let it go*. Letting go of the intended outcome is an important part of this process, because you must let go of your connection to your goal; you must learn to trust in the process and have faith that you will achieve your goal. If you don't let go, you'll allow that voice of doubt to creep into your mind, which slows down your progress.

If you allow that inner voice to express its opinion, it will second-guess any goal you set, whispering, "Is it *really* going to happen, are you *really* going to become a great vocal coach?" That will cut the connection to your creative mindset. It's like your ISP crashing while you're downloading a file—you lose the file and have to start over. Once the doubt leaves, you can pick up where you left off, but think of the time you lost because of self-doubt.

Once you've installed your program, you've got to let it run, so just let it go. Letting go doesn't mean discarding the thought and forgetting about it. It simply means that it IS installed, and you don't have to worry about it anymore, because now it's time to begin running your program every day.

How do you run or use a new program? You will run or use your program by answering the five questions and by doing activities that involve your program, all without any doubt that you will successfully accomplish your goals. Doubts = viruses. Don't get a virus! Doubt is simple to overcome. Just choose NOT to doubt, period! If you have doubt, X it out!

Once you begin running a new program, don't question *how* or *why* the program operates. You don't know exactly how and why a car runs, yet you manage to drive one, don't you? I've never questioned how Microsoft® Word allows me to write books; I just use the program and know that the words I type will appear on my screen. Focus on the goal and quit worrying about how to get to the finish line.

You'll automatically use your program, because everything you do in your life is a reflection of what you desire, who you want to become, and how you plan to reach your goals. When I installed my first program, I didn't say, "I will build my vocal coaching business" and then forget about it. I didn't think I'd magically have a business in a few weeks. I began surfing the Internet, viewing other voice-related websites, singing my vocal scales, studying books on becoming a better writer, etc. I was upgrading my computer every day by working toward my goals through research and repetition, never doubting the final outcome. I continued to study lots of voice-related material as I offered vocal lessons, knowing that my actions would expand my hard drive. My hard work allowed me to tap into the creative mindset, while leaving it up to God to guide my life toward my goals.

Two weeks after I installed my first program, a friend of mine, Jason Burnside, told me that his wife Molly designed websites. *Alakazam!* The first connection toward success was made. Your creative mindset works with the subconscious, making connections to the people, places, and situations that lead toward your goals. It brings together people of like mind, which is why Molly and I made the connection. Molly not only helped me with my website but also helped with my first book! Now she designs and maintains multiple websites for me and creates all my book covers. Whether she knows it or not, she uses her creative mindset for her designing skills.

Now it's your turn to install your first new program. Once your program is installed, begin using it and running it daily. If you feel like nothing is happening, don't fret; hang in there, because in time many positive things *will* begin happening. Time is irrelevant to God. If you don't rush the process, success will unfold.

You might be asking, "What should I install first?" I suggest starting with something small that you believe you can obtain or accomplish, something relatively easy like installing a program for "putting your band together" or "improving your Photoshop skills" to become a better artist. Once you've had success with smaller programs, you'll master larger programs with ease. We have to learn to walk before we can run.

You'll notice that one of my choices, the easel, brushes, and paint set, was a material object. If you're an artist and this was your choice, too, know that the easel won't magically appear. What will happen is that your creative mindset will figure out the best way to obtain that paint set, through your own creative talents. You may discover that one of your neighbors wants to hire someone to paint a baby room in her house with stencils along the ceiling. That little voice, known as the creative mindset, will bring that job to your attention. If you listened to your inner voice, you'll get the job, get the money, and buy the easel. Better yet, it may open up other painting opportunities.

Please don't get too caught up in materialistic programs. Material possessions will come as a result of your creative success. Focus on installing programs for using creativity to write songs or books, invent new products, boost motivation, improve your job skills, etc.

For instance, let's say you need to work out in the gym because you're on stage a lot and need to stay in shape, but you lack the motivation to exercise. You should install a new motivational program where you see yourself exercising every day and loving it.

If you feel you have writer's block, install a program to inspire writing. But I have news for you—writer's block doesn't exist. You're either bored or inspired, motivated or unmotivated. If you feel you have writer's block syndrome, install a program in which you see yourself flowing with new creative ideas, filled with inspiration and motivation. These types of programs are more fulfilling than transitory material gains.

Just remember to believe in what you program. If you don't believe, you won't achieve. Because of his lack of belief, Luke Skywalker couldn't raise his X-Wing fighter out of the water when attempting to use the Force. (Thanks to my godson Kirk Gilbert for reminding me of the name of Luke's spacecraft.) Luke thought the X-Wing was too big to lift with his mind, but in reality anything is possible when you believe!

You can stop right now and install your first program if you wish. If you're not sure what to install, move on to the next chapter where we'll discuss how to discover your creative talents.

What Do You Want To Do With Your Life?

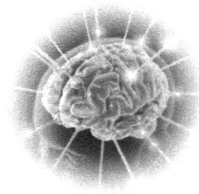

KNOW YOU'RE ANXIOUS to start your journal, but before we jump into the five questions, I want you to answer an extremely important question that will help mold your creative future and uncover your hidden talents. That question is, "What do you want to do with your life?" No, I am not reliving a Twisted Sister video. I really want to know your answer.

What we strive to accomplish in life is hard-wired to what we are passionate about, and our passion can expose our talent. We each were born with a specific talent, and I'll bet that nine out of ten times, your answer to this question will reveal that talent. What's your hobby? What do you do best?

Vocal coaching and writing are my passions; what are yours? There is nothing wrong with having more than one passion, but one will do just fine.

If you feel like you don't have any special talent, don't worry; you just need help finding it. We all have something that interests us that can be developed into an amazing talent. By asking this one simple question, you'll begin to discover your innermost passion, and once you've discovered that passion, you must bring it into your life. Immerse yourself in it, study it, live it, learn it, love it, become it! It doesn't matter what it is, just as long as it makes you happy and is a positive reinforcement for your life.

Some of you might say, "I don't have time for any hobbies because I work all day." You don't have to quit your job. (Please don't quit your job.) Just start incorporating your talent into your daily routine. If you truly desire to create a change in your life by doing what you love, you *will* find the time to enjoy your passion.

There will come a time when you have to jump off the edge to reach your goals. Jumping doesn't mean you should run out and quit your job. It just means you should begin noticing opportunities that line up with your creative goals. Then take action. When I took the leap, opportunities appeared left and right, allowing me to fulfill my creative desires.

Jumping off the edge also doesn't mean that you have to change careers to unleash your creative mindset. Maybe you love your job, so let's make your job experience even better! Taking a leap is about tapping into your creative genius and using it to better your life. Maybe you have an idea to improve your workplace but have been afraid to tell your boss. Follow your heart and spill your guts!

Maybe you're an aspiring songwriter or author and want to tap into the creative mindset to improve your lyrics or develop some new stories, but the lyrics or story ideas you generate are outside your creative norm. Take the leap; get out of your comfort zone when writing and go with the flow to further develop your writing skills.

So, tell me, what do you *really* want to do with your life? What do you *really* love doing in your spare time? There's no incorrect answer. This is the first step to discovering your talent, developing your creative skills, and tapping into the creativity stream associated with that talent.

Once you've found your talent, keep it to yourself while you're developing your skills. We all tend to get excited when we discover new things, and we want to tell everyone in the world about it. Resist the temptation.

When I decided to write my first book, *Raise Your Voice*, I spent years telling everyone, "I'm writing a book!" I got back positive responses but even more negative ones. One person said, "You'll never do it, you're just a regular guy," while another said, "You'll never make it, you aren't good enough, and chances of making it in the music business are slim to none."

Negative comments allow doubt to creep into your mind, momentarily disconnecting your link to the creative mindset. It took me more than three years to finish my first book because of self-doubt. Since then, I've learned to keep quiet and stay focused.

Negative comments can slow down your creative progress, but only if you allow those comments to break down your confidence and dissolve your motivation. You don't need that kind of negativity in your life.

If someone asks about your creative plans, it's fine to share, but it's generally best to keep them to yourself. Beware, you'll still find people with negative attitudes who don't want you to succeed. You have a choice. You can let negative comments affect you, or you can **X** out those negative thoughts and stay focused on the prize!

A LITTLE ORGANIZATION PLEASE

Once you've answered this question and discovered your talent, immediately begin using your talent to improve your creative skills. I know that other things come first in your life, such as your job and taking care of your kids, but to master your talent, you must create an organized schedule that allows you to do what you love, even if it means doing it for only fifteen minutes a day in the beginning. If it's guitar, don't "find the time" to practice, "make the time" to practice!

When you start honing your skills, don't get too excited by taking on more than you can handle at one time. I was focused on becoming a vocal coach while trying to finish my first book, film an instructional video, record audio training programs, create marketing posters, and many other tasks. Instead of finishing one task before moving on, I was overwhelmed with multiple unfinished projects.

If you can focus on one project at a time until it's finished, ALL of your projects will begin coming together quicker. Start finishing one project at a time and QUIT creating new projects before the one is finished! Practice your piano scales before writing your first song. Learn to shade your drawing before coloring.

Some people put off completing their goals by creating other tasks—seemingly important ones—to accomplish first. I plead guilty to that one. I would rearrange the music equipment in my studio instead of finishing a new series of vocal scales. If this sounds like you, please stop devising these diversionary tasks, because you're only impeding progress toward completing creative goals.

With that said, there will be times when you need to walk away from a project for a day or longer to refresh your mind. The key is to know when you're creating new tasks and when you need time to allow the creative mindset to be creative. That key is your emotions. If it feels wrong deep inside your gut to walk away from a music score you've been writing for weeks, then it is wrong. If it feels right to walk away for a day, and there's no bad emotional feeling attached to it, such as guilt, then you should walk away from the music project for a few hours or a few days until you once again feel that creative spark igniting within you. This may be the creative recharge you've needed. You'll return to the score refreshed and ready to finish your masterpiece.

Learning To Multitask

I don't like new tasks, but I do love "multitasks." However, I have a different take on the meaning of multitasking. For most people, it means doing more than one job at the same time. But you can also do one job that accomplishes more than one goal at the same time, a much better option. For example, by singing the vocal scales along with my students, I can do my daily vocal exercises while teaching voice to students, catching two fish with one hook, as it were.

Your goal is to figure out when and how to efficiently combine tasks to save time. Look for ways at work that allow you to multitask. It may be as simple as improving your typing skills at a secretarial job, thus improving your finger dexterity for guitar playing. Or you might start proofreading and correcting your email messages and become a better writer in the process.

Multitask and run your programs as much as possible to improve your talents, and always do it out of love and out of a need to share your creativity with the world. When you do what you love, and when you want to succeed to better everyone's life, then success for you is guaranteed. When we do things out of pure greed, we usually fail to succeed. Greed is a destructive seed, so don't plant it!

I love writing books and teaching workshops, sharing my knowledge with others. It's what I wanted to do with my life. Now that

I KNOW that you know what you want to do with *your* life, and you're running new programs, multitasking, and keeping a positive frame of mind, let's move on to the first of the five questions.

What Will I Do Today To Better Myself?

IMMEDIATELY AFTER you've completed the Mind/Body process, grab your journal and ask yourself, "What will I do today to better myself?" Think it over during your morning shower or while eating breakfast.

By asking this question, you'll ignite the creative spark within, inspiring focus, motivation, and daily direction. This question is your motivator for accomplishing daily goals. Don't think too hard about your answers. Just jot down whatever comes to mind. It could be as simple as:

"I'm going to do cardio this morning."

"I'll do thirty minutes of vocal exercises."

"I'll brush up on my music theory."

All three answers produce motivation and direction for your day. These particular answers run the program I installed for becoming a successful vocal coach, *without* questioning when or how I will become a vocal coach. The cardio helps my body, the vocal exercises help my voice, and the theory lessons will improve my songwriting skills.

Whatever you do today to better yourself doesn't necessarily have to be focused on your creative goals. Better yourself in ALL aspects of your life! It could include working harder at your job, playing ball with your kids after school, greeting everyone you meet with a warm smile, taking an online course related to your goals, or looking in the mirror and telling yourself you deserve success. All positive activities will improve your life and enhance the creative mindset.

It doesn't matter if you accomplish all of your written goals every day as long as you're at least focused on completing those goals every day. You *should* strive to accomplish the goals you put on paper, but don't stress yourself out if it's too hard to complete your goals on any given day. Simply change your approach. Start with easier goals that you know you can accomplish. You do feel more successful when you complete your daily goals, so start small and work up to bigger tasks.

I used to overexert myself trying to complete a too-ambitious list of daily goals. Once I realized the error of my ways, I cut my daily goal list for this question in half so that I'd complete all written goals. I wrote answers like:

"I'm submitting my book to three companies for review."
"I'll eat twice as many vegetables today."
"I'm doing the dishes for my wife."
"I'll help anyone that I see stranded on the side of the road."

With a simple approach in the beginning, you'll find that your written answers and goals are a breeze to finish.

DO UNTO OTHERS ...

Don't just focus on the tasks you write down for the day; look for new opportunities throughout the day to help other people, or "do unto others as you would have them do unto you." This act of selflessness will definitely better your own life experience.

Apply this rule to every aspect of your life. Do your job like you were the owner of the company. Help an older couple with their groceries as if they were your own grandparents. Lend a word of encouragement to every child you meet as if they were your own children.

When you express a positive attitude through your actions, do it out of love, not out of an expectation of something in return. You cannot expect to better yourself if you offer a hand to someone while thinking, "What's in this for me?" If you do good deeds just for the rewards, God won't reward you. It's not about the deeds, it's about the heart.

If someone has a flat tire on the side of the road, stop to ask if they need help or offer to change it. It could be you next. Follow what that inner voice and your heart and gut tell you about every situation. These tools were a gift given to you so you'd know what is right. Always pay attention to your emotions, and use these tools every day in order to make the right decisions. This may not seem related to unleashing your creativity, but trust me, it's all tied in.

I remember an older man who came to my door, soaking wet from the freezing rain. His car had broken down a few miles away, and he didn't have a cell phone. I was a little wary of letting him in, but I listened to my heart and gut and let him make a phone call, and then I took him to a warm rest area to wait for a tow. We talked on the way as he warmed his freezing hands on the defroster. I even offered to give him a ride to his house, which was forty-five minutes away, but he politely declined. He told me he was a retired pharmacist who had diabetes and that if he had had to go to one more house to ask for help, his legs might have given out.

Yes, I know you have to be careful; unfortunately, there *are* people who will take advantage. But, (believe it or not) we truly decide whether we are part of a victim circumstance. So listen close, and if the inner voice, heart, and gut all line up and say YES, then follow your instinct. BUT always learn as much as you can about every situation to make a logical decision.

I've lived by these rules for years, and whenever I've offered a hand to someone in need, I never expected anything in return. However, I am sure that I've been blessed for my kindness many times over, and I often wonder if I would have been blessed with all the amazing opportunities I've had thus far if I had denied others a helping hand.

Now let's discuss the consequences of being negative. As a vocal coach, I'm bombarded with requests asking for my services free of charge. I've had several emails stating, "I cannot afford you, but if you take me on as a student for free and I make it big, I'll tell them about you." They already know about me, ha-ha, so I usually hit the delete button. This is how I make my living, and although you must be willing to give something back, God never expects us to allow ourselves to be taken advantage of. You wouldn't pull into a service station and expect a free oil change, would you?

Back to the story: An old friend of mine called me up one day to congratulate me for my epic appearance on *MythBusters*. She knew I was a vocal coach and was hoping I could spend an hour with her son to give him some pointers. I said I'd be delighted. It didn't feel right charging her for my services, so I said that I'd do it as a favor. It was a great way to give back.

Because of my busy schedule, I kept putting off the lesson, and a few months passed. My friend would call me every few weeks to see if we could get together.

We finally set the lesson up for a Friday when I was heavily into writing this book. The thought of doing the lesson and walking away from finishing this book gnawed at me, because I only wanted to concentrate on finishing the book. Needless to say, I was a little aggravated.

My studio was a mess, so an hour before the lesson, I decided to break from writing and whip through the studio in a cleaning frenzy. As I swept the floor, all I thought about was the aggravation of having to stop for the voice lesson when I should be writing. Not setting a good example, am I?

My keyboard was leaning against a wall with a cover over it, and as I swept the floor like a madman, the sweeper caught the cover. Before I could even think about it, BOOM, the keyboard came tumbling over! It shattered one of the keys and could have done other damage as well. A thousand-dollar keyboard, wiped out!

I could've gotten extremely upset, but I thought to myself, "I created this terrible outcome with my sour attitude, so that's what I get for whining. If I hadn't been so negative about teaching today, this wouldn't have happened!" I took a deep breath and realized that this was an important lesson that needed to be learned.

Here's how it all panned out: I had a great time with David, and he learned a lot from the voice lesson. I got to spend some time with my friend Joyce, whom I hadn't seen in years. She tried to pay me for my services, but I refused. Knowing that David learned something valuable was payment enough.

You'll find that when you do things out of love, things have a way of working out to benefit all involved. I had been having some neck issues, and Joyce happens to be a massage therapist. So the following Monday morning I had an appointment for a massage—at no charge.

The lesson I learned that day was "you get what you give," and sometimes it happens so fast that it shocks the living crap out of you. I received a broken keyboard because of my bad attitude but instantly turned the situation around for the better, by making some friends happy.

We fall short daily; it's human nature. But if we catch our lapses, we can turn them around for the better. This story reinforces the notion that negative thoughts produce negative results. Begin paying attention to everything you do. You always have the choice to be positive or negative in any situation. My "inner voice" and feelings let me know when I am being negative. As soon as I hear it, I change my attitude.

There are times I forget to listen. Once, I needed to develop some 8 x 10 promotional pictures for a management company, so I went to a local film development store to produce them myself. The self-serve digital printing machine wouldn't read one of the pictures, so I skipped it to submit the second picture. I hit the submit button and walked away, only to come back a few minutes later, because I suddenly realized that the display looked as if it had cropped off the top of my head.

I asked the clerk if she could help me fix the picture, to which she replied, "No. You must do it at the computer." I got very aggravated and raised my voice, telling her that if she wouldn't help, I would NOT be back to pick them up. She said, "Oh, do you want to cancel the order?" I said yes and stormed off.

I found myself blaming this young lady for her incompetence when, in reality, it was my own fault for not setting up the photo correctly. I felt a big knot tightening in my gut. I felt ashamed all day long because of my reaction. If I had gone back to apologize, I could have gotten rid of that horrible feeling.

Please don't make these mistakes. Stay upbeat to better yourself every day. Always look for opportunities to do positive things in your life in order to improve yourself. Staying in a positive zone truly does ignite the creative spark within you.

Today I worked on this book to better myself, but I also ran to the grocery store to pick up some groceries to make dinner for Diana, my wife. Bringing happiness to others enhances your positive vibration to better your life. Remember, we can choose to be positive or choose to be negative, but a positive attitude creates success. As one of my favorite artists, Prince, says, "Positivity—have you had your plus sign today?"

You don't always have to feel like you must do something every day that's life-changing in order to better yourself and stimulate that creative spark within you. We all love to feel excited, but there will be many days when we feel bored or depressed because we feel as if we aren't accomplishing much. On those days, relax, read a book, or take a walk and notice all the beauty that nature has to offer.

Sometimes our brain just needs a small vacation. Breathe in fresh air while enjoying the local scenery. Whenever I fly around the world to perform on television, I always request to be brought in at least a day early so that I can simply walk around and enjoy the scenery. This stimulates my creative mindset and puts me in the zone for performing. So take a break and enjoy it!

Are you ready for the next question? Let's get "in the process" of moving on to the next chapter.

What Am I in The Process of Doing?

NOW THAT WE'RE bettering ourselves, let's focus on our talents. Whether you want to be a teacher, author, musician, painter, scientist, or just a happy couple living on a pig farm twenty miles from nowhere contemplating the meaning of life, you've got to start the process.

It has taken me years to build my voice-teaching business, but that's my fault. In the beginning, the more that I said things like, "I'm writing a book" or "I'm building a website," the slower it unfolded. There were times when it felt like I was moving backwards.

I remember complaining to a friend about what I wanted to accomplish in life and how slowly it was happening. He asked if I believed I could write a book and become a successful vocal coach. That simple question made me realize that I didn't believe it. There was always a little bit of doubt present in the back of my mind, dampening my creative mindset. I was so stressed over how I was going to print the book, build the website, and grow my student base that it impeded my progress.

My friend said, "The mental demands you are placing on yourself are the reason for your sudden halt in progress. You are spitting out words you don't mentally believe will ever come true. Words are funny little things. You could say, *I will be a vocal coach* or *I'll never be a vocal coach*, and if you aren't careful, they can both work against you due to your choice of wording and your thoughts about those words."

Saying "I'll never" is obviously negative, but saying "I will" can be just as detrimental to your creative success. If you say, "I will finish this song by the end of next week," and you have that little bit of doubt in the back of your mind, it will bring your creative mindset to a screeching halt.

He told me to start using the phrase "I am in the process" before I write down or say aloud my goals. At the time, I thought it sounded silly, and I didn't understand how that would change things. I do now. Let me explain.

We are *always* in the process of doing something, whether it takes eleven seconds, minutes, days, weeks, months, or years. When I discovered that I was "in the process" of writing a book and "in the process" of creating my website, those statements were entirely true. I WAS in the process.

Suddenly, the mental pressure of completing these tasks had disappeared, because I could be "in the process" as long as I needed to complete each task. I quit worrying about how I was going to accomplish these tasks. When my state of mind changed to being "in the process," everything began falling into place.

A few years later, another friend pointed out that best-selling author/marketing guru, Joe Vitale is an advocate for "in the process." My friend then suggested I check out some of Joe's books. I have since become a huge fan. Ironically, I come to find out that Joe is a fan of my singing books! Wow, the Mindset connection at work once again!

What are you in the process of doing right now? Are you in the process of becoming a better guitar player? Are you in the process of finishing your record? Designing a computer game? Becoming an art teacher?

Everything you do in life is a process, from the process of eating your breakfast, brushing your teeth, going to your job, picking your kids up from school, to developing a new career. If you want to become a piano teacher, write in your journal, "I am in the process of becoming a piano teacher" or "I am in the process of mastering the Hanon scales so I can teach them to others."

Your journal is an extremely powerful tool. Don't use the journal like Facebook to write out every little boring detail of your life. In other words, don't jot down, "I am in the process of taking my shower." The journal is for bigger goals, such as focusing on writing a No. 1 hit song or becoming a published author.

Once you've written down a few answers, become part of the process. Start working on that hit song by writing out lyrics or playing some chords on your guitar. If you're an aspiring artist, your process could be taking more art classes at a local college or hauling an easel out into the middle of the forest to draw some nature scenes. Immerse yourself in all things related to your process.

As you go through your day, ask yourself *what* you're in the process of doing at that moment. When you think about your goals, remember to add that you are "in the process" of accomplishing each goal. Write down your answers in your diary, and then be in the process!

We are always in the process of doing something, and many days your "process" won't be something exciting. But as long as it produces a good feeling inside, it is important. Some of your answers might be, "I am in the process of getting together with my parents for dinner" or "I am in the process of moving" or "I am in the process of reading the want ads in order to find a better job." These are still great answers, because they lead you to complete a task, and nine times out of ten, creative people fail because they become too lazy to finish tasks. When you're a student of Mindset, there's no room for procrastination.

PROCESS DEADLINES

I know I said that being in the process allows a lot of freedom as far as time constraints. But that doesn't mean you should become lazy (remember, no procrastination). I think setting "process" goals is extremely important. If you are in the process of writing a book, you should seriously consider setting a solid deadline. Make it a reasonable amount of time. Could you finish your first book in six months? If so, and if you started on January 1, write in your journal, "I am in the process of completing my book by July 1." This instills a subconscious motivational drive to complete your book. Now that you are in the process of accomplishing your goals, let's discuss ways to keep the process positive.

BUILDING THE POSITIVE/RELEASING THE NEGATIVE

It can be tough to stay positive throughout the day. I understand that some days seem to drag and leave you wondering if you've accomplished anything. Such days can leave you feeling defeated. But you still have the choice to stay positive and block negativity from clouding your mind with doubt.

Your words affect every aspect of your life and shape your future. Always choose your words wisely. If you have an illness such as diabetes, but you also have a very optimistic attitude about your health, I still think it wise not to write in your journal, "I am in the process of beating diabetes!" Although you are upbeat about your situation, the word *diabetes* still reflects a certain negative view about your state of health. When we think of that word, we think of illness. I understand you must use the word, but it would be better to write, "I am in the process of total healing" or "I am in the process of becoming healthy," because these are positive ways to use words without referring to your illness. I bring this up because I know many famous musicians who have dealt with illnesses but who have continued to tour successfully. By not focusing on their illness, apart from taking care of themselves as they should, they still give amazing performances night after night.

This rule applies to any process. If you want to drop a few pounds to look better on stage, and you've installed a weight loss program, don't say, "I am in the process of losing weight." "Losing" has a negative vibration. We're not losers, we're winners! "I am in the process of becoming healthier and thinner" is a better way to state the same goal.

Similarly, if you want to quit your job and find a better one, you shouldn't say, "I am in the process of quitting my job," because "quitting" has a negative vibration. "I am in the process of rising to a higher position in my field" is a wiser way to state your goal.

If you've left your job, don't state, "I'll never go back to my old job," because that statement keeps your focus on your old job. When I left my construction job, I kept saying, "I'm never going back to construction," and all it did was slow down the process of becoming a successful vocal coach.

Get the picture? Now get "in the process" and always state your goals in the best positive light that you can. If you have the slightest inkling that your answer or phrase might be connected in any way to a negative thought or emotion, immediately find a new way to phrase your desires and answers!

ACCEPT AND LEARN FROM LIFE'S LESSONS

Throughout our lives, we've all faced obstacles that impact our process, including health issues, financial decisions, moral issues, and emotional connections that lead to ups and downs that test our belief system. But obstacles also can be beneficial, because they can help us learn and grow, which develops character.

If we approach any obstacle negatively, we won't learn from the situation. We'll become stagnant and bring the process to a halt. Success will elude us. The hardest part of being in the process is letting go and letting God take over. If we try to control the process, we'll only become static. It's not up to us; it's up to God.

I didn't get mad when it took nearly four years to write my first book, *Raise Your Voice*. Once I realized that I was my own problem, I let go, installed my programs, and continued to be in the process of writing until *Raise Your Voice* was released. I continued participating and working toward that process, even when obstacles slowed me down. If you are in the process of writing that great song, and the lyrics aren't flowing, don't get mad and give up. Simply trust in the process, and the lyrics will come to you in time.

THE OUTCOME OF OUR PROCESS

Many times we have preconceived notions of what we think the outcome of "the process" should be. This refers to ALL our programs and processes, from being in the process for finding a new job, to the way we hear a particular song being written in our mind, to which stage we feel we should be performing on. Maybe you don't get the job you wanted as a choir director at a local college. Maybe the song didn't turn out the way you envisioned. Maybe your band didn't make it to the main stage and got bumped to stage B. But maybe your creative future would have been stifled as the choir director at that local college; maybe now it will include an even better job down the line than the one you so badly wanted. Maybe your band wasn't ready for the main stage. Maybe performing on stage B reduced stress and allowed the band to cut loose and gain some confidence. Don't let seemingly negative events ruin your creative mindset. Allow yourself to be in the process, and things will work out the way that is best for you. It's about trust.

Trust may seem like a hard pill to swallow, but it's the only way to accomplish your goals. I promise that if you live your life to the fullest in every waking moment, praise and thank God, and stay positive, you will reach your goals.

Let's open up our journals and add a goal-setting process. If you are going to apply for a job promotion so that you can make more money to set up your home studio, you should write, "I am in the process of getting a promotion at work." Write it in your journal, and then mentally repeat, "I am in the process of getting a job promotion" until you see it, feel it, and believe it!

Do you want to stimulate your creative mindset to improve your return rate? When writing, "I am in the process of getting a job promotion at work," draw a cartoon of you in your new job position or create some symbol that relates to your new job. If you work in the mailroom but want to program computers, draw a little picture of a computer in your journal. Close your eyes and see that symbol on your mind monitor. Doodle a little cartoon of your new home studio, knowing it's one of your end goals.

When you finally trust and believe it will happen, it *will* happen in the way that best suits you! Do you remember in **Field of Dreams** when that voice whispered, "If you build it, they will come"? Trust and it will happen.

Remember, if you don't get that promotion, don't get upset. Let it go, and trust in the process. Let go of all those negative emotions;

you don't need them. There's a reason for everything. Maybe you are destined to get an even better promotion!

I know how powerful doubt can be when things don't seem to go our way. I had my doubts on my first television show until I realized that I was in the process of being successful on camera. I didn't do very well during rehearsal, so doubt slipped into my mind. I was very nervous afterwards. So I went to the restroom to be alone. I was standing at the urinal, and that little voice said, "Drop to your knees and pray right now and you WILL do amazing in the show!" What do you think I did? I listened to that voice, and I dropped to my knees, praying. Then I KNEW I was in the process of succeeding on the show. I wound up giving an amazing performance because I trusted in the process and believed in God.

That experience helped me overcome my doubts. If you have doubt in the back of your mind, you must immediately get rid of it! If you catch yourself saying, "I know I'm not going to get that promotion" or "I can't afford a new microphone so I'll never finish my demo," you must IMMEDIATELY turn those statements around and say, "I am in the process of getting that promotion!" or "I am in the process of getting my microphone!" Eliminate those negative words from your vocabulary. Watch the words that come out of your mouth! Words are power, and they form your future. You'll have what you say, whether good or bad.

From now on, you are NEVER allowed to finish any negative sentence. The next time you catch yourself saying, "I can't, I'll never, I won't," stop and change that sentence into a positive one. Remember, you are "in the process" of accomplishing your goal or achieving your dream.

Are you starting to get the picture? It's about a total creative mindset of positive reinforcement. Now let's talk about tapping into our creative ideas.

Do I Have Any New Ideas?

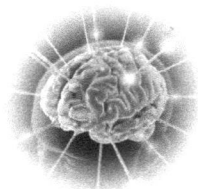

THIS NEXT BIG QUESTION is **the** secret to tapping into the creative mindset. God made all of us creative beings. We can create new ideas, new job opportunities, new books, new songs, and even new inventions. You can easily access thousands of new ideas.

When you ask, "Do I have any new ideas?" you are reaching into that giant toolbox of creativity to find the exact tools needed for you to create your own success. You are asking the manager of the knowledge bank if you can make a withdrawal. Ask this question and let it go; do not search for the answers. You'll receive answers when you are ready to receive them. New ideas will come to you in the blink of an eye. They are always there, patiently waiting in the back of your mind for you to find them, whispering, "I've got a new idea, how about ..."

Sometimes you'll ask if you have any new ideas, and the answers will instantly appear, while other times the answers you're looking for will take hours, days, even weeks before they surface. Bottom line: Don't force creative ideas; allow them to surface in due time.

This question asks your creative mindset to start the process of getting the creative juices flowing in order to bring forth great ideas. What new ideas can we conceive? Anything you can dream, you can create.

New ideas for books, songs, and products pop into my mind all the time. I even dream ideas, which is why I keep my journal beside my bed, just in case I wake up in the middle of the night with a new idea. I've had too many great ideas pop up during sleep, only to wake up saying, "I'll remember that idea in the morning." Guess what? I've never remembered any of my nighttime ideas unless I wrote them down in my journal!

ASKING SPECIFIC QUESTIONS

If you have a specific problem that needs to be solved, such as finding that golden chord progression to finish your musical masterpiece, take out your journal, and under your "New Ideas" header write, "What chords complete this song?" Close your journal and repeat your question out loud three times in a row, and then let it go. Always keep your journal close by (and possibly your guitar or keyboard), because the answer *will* pop up out of nowhere. Once the answer comes to you, write it down in your journal underneath your question.

I use this technique for all sorts of questions I have, even to remember names of songs. I write it in my journal, say out loud three times, "What is the name of the song by so and so?", and then let it go. Before I know it, the name of the song pops into my mind.

The creative mindset is ready to give you tons of ideas freely; all you have to do is be ready and willing to accept them. How do you think we've advanced so rapidly with our technology over the years? Aliens? Well, maybe, but that's not my field of expertise. We had great minds ready and willing to accept new ideas from the creative mindset. An inquisitive person sought to solve some problem, let it go, and then, *BOOM!* Out of nowhere the answer came to that person.

LEARNING TO LISTEN

Have you ever heard the saying, "If it had been a snake it would have bitten me"? When you install new programs into your mind and run them daily, your subconscious mind and creative mindset will create coincidences to lead you toward your goal. Most of us stumble right past those coincidences and don't think twice about making the connection. Pay close attention to everything in your life that catches your eye. These coincidences are now happening for a reason. The creative mindset is speaking to you, so always pay attention! Listen to that little voice in the back of your mind, follow your gut feeling, listen to your heart. The more you pay attention, the easier it is to follow the directions given to you by the creative mindset.

One day after leaving a store, I loaded my trunk and pushed the buggy into the car slot next to mine. The buggy area was about thirty feet across the lot, but I was feeling lazy. That little voice said, "Hey, Jaime, put the buggy where it belongs." I ignored it, knowing I should have listened. I got into my car and began backing out. In my rearview mirror I could see the buggy rolling out into the lane of traffic. I put my car into park, hopped out and put the buggy where it belonged. The little voice then said, "You better start paying attention when I'm talking to you." I know this story might seem like an insignificant example, but all our insights are important. That shopping cart might have dented someone's car. The lesson I learned was that I need to follow my own advice and listen to my inner voice.

PUTTING YOUR COMPUTER IN SLEEP MODE

You can dream answers to questions while sleeping! Many a great person in history has found the answer to a problem while dreaming. Many life-saving medicines were the result of a dream. Countless musicians confess to having dreamed entire songs. Dreams are powerful tools for accessing our creativity.

Keep your journal beside your bed. When you dream it, you can write it down in the middle of the night. Never think, "I'm too tired to deal with it now, I'll remember in the morning." Nine times out of ten, you won't.

I once dreamt the most beautifully orchestrated song I'd ever heard. I got out of bed to work it out on my keyboard, and when I tried to play the keyboard, I couldn't hear any sound. I suddenly realized that I was still dreaming. That was enough to wake me up, but then I thought to myself, "I'm too tired. If it's that good a song, I'll remember it in the morning." I went back to sleep. But the song wouldn't leave my mind, so I got up, went to my keyboard, and again there was no sound. I instantly woke up from the dream, and for the second time, I thought, "I'm too tired. I'll remember it in the morning." You can guess the outcome. Of course, I didn't remember it the next morning. I haven't remembered a single note from that score.

My subconscious was bound and determined to get me out of my bed and motivated to play what the creative mindset was giving me, but I wouldn't have any part of it. Apparently, I didn't want it badly enough. I lost the privilege to be the one to write that song. To this day, I still haven't written anything that I feel comes close to the beauty I heard that night.

The point I'm trying to make is that you must always listen to your dreams, and then write them down or record them immediately. Don't be lazy; get up out of bed and write it down! Do whatever you have to do to make sure you don't lose those gifts from God.

DAYDREAMING NEW IDEAS

You can also daydream ideas throughout your day. Too many children were scolded for daydreaming, both at home and at school. Adults need to realize that daydreamers are the answer to our world's future. Daydreaming is a way of connecting with our "inner child" and believing with absolute faith.

If you have a problem that needs to be solved, create a mini-movie in your mind, pretending to discover the answer. You could be Indiana Jones discovering the answer in an old tomb. If you're an author and need an idea for a story, daydream it. That's how my writing partner, Daniel Middleton, and I produce fiction stories for 711 Press. We dream up these amazing stories from our creative mindsets.

If you're an artist, visualize yourself painting on a blank canvas. You can use the daydreaming technique for any situation. Some of our greatest inventors, musicians, and businessmen are players of this game. Every idea begins as a dream.

We've mainly focused on problem-solving ideas, but you should know that a great idea doesn't have to occur out of "needing" to solve a problem. Maybe you've watched some infomercial for an abdominal exercise machine, and later on that day an idea for a better abdominal machine suddenly popped into your mind. You better write that idea down and act on it before someone beats you to it!

ACT ON YOUR IDEAS

Once new ideas begin flowing, the creative juices will continue to flow until you've had your fill. What you do with these new ideas will determine if you are going to become successful through your creativity. When you come up with an idea, you need to act on it immediately, because every human has the same gift—the ability to dream up ideas and tap into them. It doesn't matter if your idea is the next abdominal exercise machine, next Mona Lisa, next "Stairway to Heaven," or the next top-selling book on Amazon. Listen to your gut and act on it now.

"How do we know the difference between a random thought popping into our head and our creative mindset nudging us in the right direction?" To differentiate between that inner voice and the ticker tape playing in your head, continually ask all five questions day after day. The flashes of genius you receive from the creative mindset happen more often with repetition of the five questions and the Mind/Body process. Those gut feelings will become stronger, and the whispering inner voice will become louder, clearer, and more recognizable.

One day long, long ago, I was on my way to see my future wife, Diana. I decided to take a different exit to get to her house. I heard this little voice whisper, "Don't take that exit." I ignored it only to hear it once again just before I took the exit. The second time the voice was a little louder and said, "DON'T take this exit!" I started getting nervous, and I got a sick feeling in my stomach after hearing the voice a second time, but I still ignored it and all the physical signs.

At the bottom of the exit ramp, I looked left and right for traffic, and then proceeded to turn right. BAM, out of nowhere a dark blue car appeared, and I crashed right into the side of it. That little voice in the back of my head replied, "I told you so." That was God trying to protect me from a wreck.

I hope you will learn a valuable lesson from my unfortunate experience. Listen to that inner voice every moment of your life! Once you put your trust and faith in God, you are always connected to the creative mindset, the ultimate ISP. Open up and trust to start receiving information.

Don't Just Stand There, Do Something!

Don't sit back waiting to receive a new idea, thinking, "I am in the process." ***Participate*** in the process. Be ready to ***work*** toward your goals! If you program your mind to better your life and are in the process of becoming a lead vocalist, you'd better take action in that direction, because an amazing singing voice doesn't just happen.

Tell yourself, "I am in the process of becoming an amazing singer." Ask if you have any new ideas to progress toward developing your voice. If you get the sudden idea to buy a newspaper, and an ad jumps out at you, read it. If the ad says, "Get a year's worth of vocal lessons for the price of six months," you'd better think about signing up! And if an ad doesn't jump out at you, take the initiative and pick up books or videos on vocal technique. That's how to be "in the process" of becoming an amazing singer.

Once you're part of the process, coincidences will begin to occur frequently. This is not magic mumbo jumbo; it's our intelligence taking the lead and revealing situations in our lives that guide us toward success.

Involve yourself in many goal-related activities. That will be enjoyable, because it's doing what you love, which makes it easy to be in the process. When I wanted to learn how to improve my singing voice, I studied tons of voice-related books, videos, and training programs, including other voice-related subjects such as breathing technique, sinus and allergy cures, foot reflexology, and positive mental reinforcement techniques.

I asked if I had any new ideas to improve singing technique. That inner voice whispered, "You should create your own vocal program." So I installed a program to create a vocal method and worked hard to develop that method. My desire to create it was so intense that I created one of the most successful vocal training methods available today, known as the Isolation Method. If I had daydreamed about it, let it go, and then gotten lazy, not bothering to participate in the creation process, I might not have reached the success I'm having now! Install your programs today, become part of the process, ask for new ideas, and get busy changing your life!

Once creative ideas begin flowing, don't forget to be thankful for receiving them. God hates pride, so always be humble and remember where these ideas are coming from. Ideas are wonderful gifts from God, and when you receive a gift you should thank the one who gave it to you. Speaking of being thankful, I believe it's time for the next question in the Mindset program: "What am I thankful for?"

What Am I Thankful For?

THERE'S A SECRET WAY to strengthen your connection to your creative mindset. The secret is acknowledging your accomplishments by being thankful for everything you've received. Throughout the day, ask yourself, "What am I thankful for?"

Be thankful for everything you've been blessed with, even the simplest things. The more thankful you are, the more successful you'll become. For instance, I was about to leave the house one day to deposit two checks into my bank account, and I happened to forget my hat. I went back into the bedroom to get it, and there on the bed lay my checks. I would've gone all the way to the bank without the checks if not for one simple thing. What did I do? I thanked God for telling me that I forgot my hat!

Be thankful for your health, wealth, happiness, success, for the song you write, the novel you create, the picture you paint, and everything you have at this moment in your life. If you cannot be thankful for what you have right now, how can you possibly expect to receive more? A buddy of mine asked his company for a raise. I overheard the boss saying, "Why should I give him a raise? He doesn't appreciate what he has now!" Being thankful now boosts success power later!

Even when the cards seem stacked against you, you can always find a blessing. Obstacles in life are great opportunities for personal growth. Look for the opportunity in every situation. I was in a wreck that totaled my vehicle. It was a bad experience, but I am very thankful to be alive.

BE THANKFUL FOR OTHERS' SUCCESS

Being thankful for others' success enhances your connection to your creative mindset, thus boosting your own success. If you show jealousy, anger, or disdain over another's success, you'll only create negativity in your own life, diminishing your creative mindset.

A friend told me that her vocal coach was touring with a famous singer, making thousands of dollars just keeping the singer's voice intact. I first thought, "Why is he on the road instead of me?" Then I paused and said to my friend, "Good for your vocal coach. He deserves it." I thanked God for the vocal coach's success and prayed he'd receive more blessings.

To boost your creative mindset, be thankful for all people, even those you're not in sync with. If someone rubs you the wrong way, forgive and bless them, mentally sending them love. Be thankful you've released any negative feelings toward them. Resentment only corrupts your mental hard drive.

Bottom line: Always be thankful for what you have, what you receive, your health, your current wealth, and your current success in life; be thankful for your fellow man (and woman) as well, and be thankful for every opportunity you're given to help someone in need.

And FYI—being thankful now for a memory from ten years ago works just as well as it would have back then. Be thankful for the past, present, and future. If you recall your fifth-grade music teacher spending an afternoon helping you master the fingerings on your saxophone because you were falling behind the rest of the class, and you didn't thank the teacher back then, thank him or her now and thank God for presenting that opportunity for creative growth! If you feel good inside after giving God thanks, you are boosting your positivity. Now it's time for the last question, which is, "What did I do today to better myself?"

What Did I Do Today To Better Myself?

WE'VE REACHED the final question. The previous chapters have presented you with the tools needed to accomplish your goals. Now it's time for reflection.

What did *you* do today to better yourself? Recap the entire day, because the answers are everywhere. As you reflect at the end of the day, review your answers to your first question, "What will I do today to better myself?" When reviewing, checkmark everything you accomplished that day, because each is something you've done to better yourself.

Checkmarking the list is a mental motivational tool that will subconsciously drive you harder to complete all the tasks that you set for yourself in the morning. If you didn't complete your daily list, don't stress. It will happen. You'll eventually be driven to complete all the tasks you set, no matter how big or small. You'll no longer fall into the category of people who give up easily. You will begin to thrive and not merely survive.

Once you've finished reflecting upon your day, repeat the Mind/Body process before going to bed. You can use the Mind/Body process not only to fully awaken and energize your mind and body for the day, but also to become relaxed for a great night's rest. The Mind/Body process defragments/deletes the entire day's mental junk in preparation for supercharged, idea-filled dreams.

One final thought before moving on. If you don't answer all five questions every day, don't worry about it. This is not about creating answers; it's about letting the answers surface in your mind as they come to you. If you don't have new ideas every day, do not worry yourself sick. Answers will emerge from the creative mindset when needed.

Go ahead, pat yourself on the back. Now that you've finished one complete day of the Mindset program, you deserve it. Now all you need to do is go to bed, get some sleep, wake up tomorrow morning, and repeat the entire program. That's the Mindset program in a nutshell. Take the Mindset challenge, stick to the entire program, and get ready for some fun-filled adventures that are guaranteed to bring new creative ideas and more success into your life. Don't forget to share your adventures with your fellow Mindset users on the Mindset message board.

Before ending, I'd like to share a few personal stories about how this program has worked in my life to prove that Mindset works!

Mindset Works!

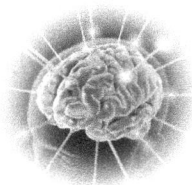

HOPE THAT YOU ARE making the Mindset program a part of your daily life, because Mindset works! I've shared with you how I've been blessed with singing, writing, and performing success, but here are a few stories to give you a bit more insight into how to apply the program to your own life. These aren't all life-changing stories, but I believe they prove that this program does work.

THE TIME I LOST MY VOICE

Years ago, I forgot the words to a song during a performance and froze up on stage in front of an entire audience. The incident scarred me to the point that every time the date for an upcoming performance drew near, I'd get symptoms of laryngitis a week before the show and would have to cancel the gig. If I had to do the gig, I'd get stage fright.

When I realized that I had programmed myself with fear, I defragmented my mind and installed a program to rebuild my vocal confidence. I created the perfect performance on my mental monitor, visualizing the approval of the crowd, and I watched as every person in the audience stood up to give me a standing ovation. As I heard the applause, I felt an immense happiness and satisfaction from doing a great job. I felt as if my voice was floating up out of me on every single note. I visualized people commenting on how I had touched them emotionally. That's all it took! The next time I performed, I felt healthy, my voice was extremely powerful, and I regained my self-confidence. I've used this approach with several singers who had to record in the studio while sick, and it's worked every time.

THE SOLUTION IN A FLASH

I had just launched my first website when I realized how much capital was needed to get the voice-teaching business running smoothly. Like every other working adult, I had a full-time job, which supplied just enough money to cover my mortgage and monthly bills, so I just couldn't spare the money needed for the site and didn't want to take out a business loan.

I defragmented my hard drive and then installed a financial program, mentally repeating, "The money I need will come" as I installed the program. After I installed the program, I let it go. Within two weeks I received a letter in the mail from a company that owed me some residuals I had forgotten about. The amount was more than I needed to launch the business. I was very thankful for this blessing.

THE GLASS ALWAYS SHATTERS!

My allergies have affected my singing voice over the years, but I can always count on my voice to be there come performance time. One particular time, I was sick in bed for six days straight with a 102° temperature. On the morning of the seventh day, I had to perform for my first Japanese television show, but I still had no voice. That morning, I installed a program for a great performance. That afternoon, I walked up onto the stage, throat completely raw, and the moment I opened my mouth, all the notes were there.

I have since installed a new program that assures my voice is always there when I perform. When I hit the stage, whether I am singing, breaking glass, or conducting a vocal workshop, I can always count on my voice. Even when I am not in great voice, within a few minutes of performing, my voice feels great!

With that said, I did fail on one show, though I wouldn't consider it a failure. The goal was three glasses. Not a problem, as three in a row is sort of my trademark. However, as I walked on stage in front of a live audience, I was given only sixty seconds, which was near impossible in the setting. I panicked and didn't focus. I threw my own Mindset program out the window. However, I didn't feel bad about it and actually learned from the experience. We will have bumps in the road, but remember, we can ALWAYS learn something positive from every experience.

THE IDEA GENERATOR IS ALWAYS ON!

Do I ever have writer's/creator's block? Never! Once you open the floodgates to creativity, the waters run wild. I'm continually asking the five questions, which send a ton of new product, book, and marketing ideas flooding into my mind. It works like this when I write music as well. In fact, I never write lyrics, because I just think about the song and the words begin to flow. If I let them write themselves, they flow like gushing water.

Many people I've met become inspired to write books, create products, or creatively expand their business because my creative mindset releases ideas that help them begin finding their way to success. I freely offer these ideas, and I am thankful to do so.

I receive new ideas every day. Whenever I watch a commercial, I ask myself, "Do I have any ideas for a better product than this one?" I usually get an answer. You can see many of these new ideas and endorsements unfold at jaimevendera.com.

HOW WAS THIS BOOK WRITTEN?

When I began writing this book, I looked to God for guidance. I tapped into the creative mindset and allowed the ideas to flow. I wrote the first edition of this book in three days. It was a 72-hour writing frenzy. I couldn't stop until the floodgates closed.

MY ROUNDTABLE OF MENTORS

This is actually a bonus "mental technique" I've used for years. After I programmed myself to be a vocal coach, I began visualizing myself sitting at a round table with all the singers that influenced me over the years. I would ask each singer questions about the singing voice. I kept my diary with me to write down new voice-related ideas that would arise from these roundtable meetings, and I continued to use this process during the entire time writing my first book, *Raise Your Voice*.

Many of the answers from these conversations made their way into my first book. Here is where it gets interesting. All of the singers that sat at my table have become personal friends of mine. They call me up to chat, ask for help, and offer advice, and they've helped me make connections in the music world to further my career. More interesting is that most of these singers found me, rather than me seeking them out.

You can use my roundtable method to help advance your career as well. If you want to be a fantasy-fiction author, visualize all your favorite authors sitting at the table helping you plot your masterpiece. Invite anyone you wish to your roundtable. I guess you now know that I am "mental" over being mental, ha-ha.

NOW IT'S TIME TO MAKE MINDSET WORK FOR YOU!

Through the years, I've taught the Mindset program to countless people, helping them find and hone their creative talents. I guarantee there is a talent inside you that can bring success into your life.

There is nothing new about the information in this book. It's just my particular slant on the accumulated knowledge collected from my subconscious, filtered through my personal life experiences. All the information already exists. We just need to access it. When we access the massive bank of knowledge known as the creative mindset, we present our findings through our own personal filtered view of knowledge, based on our own life experiences. Now it's your turn to tap into the creative mindset.

Make the Mindset program part of your daily life. At times it may feel as if you don't have the mental drive needed to do the Mindset program every day, but once you are serious about making it part of your life, it will become second nature. You'll only fail to achieve your goals if you fail to participate in the process, or if you try to control the final outcome. You'll only create roadblocks by trying to figure out the how, when, why, and where success is going to happen, instead of letting go and trusting in God to provide.

The strongest vibration is love; so when you can let go, trust in God, and do everything out of love, it will all fall into place. Begin making daily prayer as common as breathing, do the Mind/Body process day and night, answer those five simple questions daily, and allow God to do the rest.

Have fun and enjoy the Mindset game. God wants us to be happy when we play the game so that we can serve our higher purpose, help to better this world, and live an abundant life. In the words of Joel Osteen, "Live your best life NOW!"

My main intention in writing this book was to guide you toward God, spark your creativity, and motivate you to achieve your goals. I hope my plan worked. Don't forget to share your wonderful Mindset experiences on the Mindset message board. Just remember, it all comes from God.

I really hope you've enjoyed this book. I loved writing it. I want to give thanks to all of you for reading this book and a special thanks to my Lord and Savior, Jesus Christ, for showing me the way. See you next book, as I'm sure I'll write another. May all your dreams come true!

God Bless,

Jaime Vendera

Appendix A: Putting it All Together

T HE FOLLOWING IS a quick review guide for the Mindset program:

1. **Oxygenate the body** – Begin the Mind Body Process first thing upon waking in the morning. Begin by taking several deep breaths through your nose and exhaling through your mouth, and then apply the Extreme Breathing method.

2. **Prayer** – Begin with your prayers. Connect to God and start your day right.

3. **Energize the body** – Tense and release the muscles while allowing a tingling sensation to cover your body, starting at your toes and working upwards until you reach the top of your head. Allow all tension to leave your body. Light your body sparkler and allow the stagnant energy to disappear.

4. **Using your monitor** – Close your eyes, visualizing the following colored numbers: **RED 7, ORANGE 6, YELLOW 5, GREEN 4, BLUE 3, INDIGO 2, VIOLET 1.** Refer to the back cover of this book for a visual guide.

5. **Balance the left and right brain** – Defragment your computer for four minutes by putting your hands on the sides of your temples and feeling for the pulse on each temple. Keep your mind blank. If anything pops into your mind or on your mind monitor, delete it or allow it to float away.

6. **Install new programs** – Using the four-minute miracle, install new programs. As you visualize, use all five senses and attach emotions to the program as you see your goal completed. After four minutes, let it go and KNOW that it WILL be accomplished. Do NOT try to figure out how it will happen. Have faith. Let it go, and the creative mindset will

make the necessary connections needed to bring success into your life! Only install one new program per day!

7. **Do what you love and organize** – Do more of what you love every day. My love is singing, so I sing every day and teach voice. Organize your life and finish your goals one at a time. Organization is the key.

8. **What will I do today to better myself?** Every morning when you wake, ask yourself, "What will I do today to better myself?" Maybe you'll begin writing that book you've been planning to write for two years, or visit your grandmother whom you haven't seen for three months. It's not only about the choices directly aimed at you but also about bringing joy into other people's lives, which will help you grow as an individual and enhance other people's lives. It's the ripple effect. Skip a stone on a lake and watch how the water forms tiny ripples that expand and affect the entire area of the lake. If you skip many stones, the ripples multiply. Whenever you create more positivity in your life, the effects expand and affect everyone involved. Give yourself some direction.

9. **I am in the process** – What are YOU in the process of accomplishing? Write it, record, it, contemplate it, and DO IT throughout the day! Build the positive and release the negative. You are always in the process of doing something great. Turn ALL negative statements around into positive statements.

10. **New ideas** – Pay attention to all of your thoughts, especially the thoughts that stand out and produce those gut feelings and whispers in the back of your mind. They are there to give you guidance. Follow all of your hunches and act immediately on them. Write them down, record them, contemplate them, and trust them. Become them.

11. **What am I thankful for?** – Give thanks to God each day for the beautiful weather, the roof over your head, your new career, that unexpected check, your health, for all of the

positive things that happen throughout your day. How many things can YOU be thankful for every day? Give thanks and write them down to keep track of the countless things you can be thankful for. Count your blessings, literally! Starting today I want you to notice all the great things happening in your life, all your blessings and accomplishments, and give thanks for them. Pray every morning and thank God for another day that you have experienced. Be thankful for your health, wealth, and success. Keep in mind that there are different levels of health, wealth, and success. Just because you aren't a millionaire doesn't mean you shouldn't give thanks for a minimum wage job. That job helped put food on your table. If you are recovering from some illness, be thankful that you are becoming healthy. If you are sick right now, give thanks that you are still alive and working through the situation and are in the process of healing. If you are truly thankful, God will reward you with more wealth, better health, and far greater success. Don't focus on what you don't have; be thankful for what you do have! Give thanks before meals. There are plenty of people in the world who go hungry. Be thankful that you are provided for. Give thanks for your family and all of your personal relationships. At the end of the day, before you retire to bed, count the blessings that you gave thanks for throughout your day. Each "thank you" produces a ripple of positivity on the big ocean of life. Are you ready to ride the wave? Even Job from the Bible was thankful after losing his family and wealth. He still gave thanks to God and was rewarded many times over for his faithfulness.

12. **What did I do today to better myself?** — At the end of the day, you must take time to reflect back on your accomplishments. This lets you know that you are on the path to your dreams and goals. All positive things great and small bring you closer to your goals! When you lie

down at night, ask yourself, "What did I do today to better myself?" Don't ever waste a single day. You should always have some direction in the morning and positive reflection at night, no matter how small. Maybe today you just picked up a fresh bouquet of flowers for your spouse to brighten up your home. That is still a great "positive direction." Acknowledge it. All things positive bear fruit. I hope you are inspired to be positive and take control of your life.

Appendix B: Suggested Reading

The Bible

The Attractor Factor and The Awakening Course
By Dr. Joe Vitale

Become a Better You & Your Best Life Now
By Joel Osteen

The Genesis Prayer
By Jeffrey Meiliken

God's Creative Power Gift Collection
By Charles Capps

The Lost Mode of Prayer
By Gregg Braden

The Miracle Prayer
By Mitchell Gibson

The Moses Code
By James F. Twyman

The Power of Your Subconscious Mind
By Joseph Murphy, Ph.D., D.D

The Prayer of Jabez
By Bruce Wilkinson

The Seven Great Prayers
By Paul McManus

Ten Prayers God Always Says Yes To
By Anthony Destefano

Jaime Vendera is the author of a variety books and one of the most sought-after vocal coaches on the planet. Using the methods that he created, Jaime turned his two-octave range into six octaves with massive decibels of raw vocal power that enabled him to set a world record, shattering glass with his voice. When singers need more vocal range, power, and projection, or need to build up vocal stamina to perform every night, they call Jaime Vendera. Jaime states that "none of this would have been possible without God."

Ben Thomas of Dweezil Zappa says that Jaime is the "Mr. Miyagi" of vocal coaches, while Mat Devine of Kill Hannah considers him more of a "Yoda." James LaBrie of Dream Theater said, "Because of my lessons with Jaime, my voice is feeling and sounding better than it has in twenty years. I am spot-on every night. He is the Vocal Guru." Myles Kennedy of Alter Bridge said, "One time during a tour, I was so sick I could barely make it through the set. It looked as if we were going to have to cancel the next show. Jaime spent some time giving me some tips that helped me regain my voice. By the next night, I was able to perform the show. He is fantastic! *Raise Your Voice Second Edition* is THE book for singers. I recommend his books and his private instruction to ALL singers."

Learn more about Jaime at jaimevendera.com and buildabettervoice.com.